Exploring Art Masterpieces

With Young Learners

Pull-Out Posters of Four Great Works With Hands-on Activities Across the Curriculum

by Rhonda Graff Silver

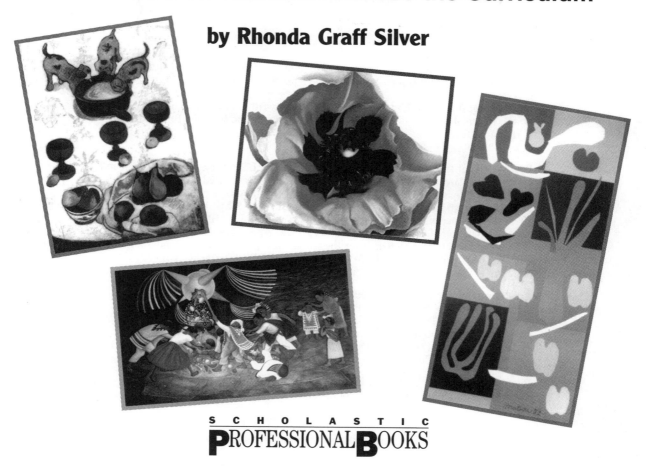

SCHOLASTIC
PROFESSIONAL BOOKS

NEW YORK ◆ TORONTO ◆ LONDON ◆ AUCKLAND ◆ SYDNEY

Dedication

To my loving parents, Joan and Stan Graff,
my aunt, Anna Vener...
And to my truly special, supportive husband, Scott
and our precious son, Craig Matthew
—with love

Special thanks to...

the children and parents at Woodglen Elementary School, New City, New York, who shared room 113 with me... Ruth Gerard, my friend and teaching assistant... Marji Crandall Siegel, Pat Santanello, Karin Damtoft, Danielle Helmers, and Dr. Wally Dimson for being part of our team... and my mother for reading and rereading. A very special thank-you to Liza Charlesworth, a supportive and encouraging editor.

Poetry "What Is Red" from HAILSTONES AND HALIBUT BONES by Mary O'Neill and Leonard Weisgard. Copyright © 1961 by Mary LeDue O'Neill; used by permission of Doubleday, a division of Bantam Doubleday Dell Publishing Group., Inc. "Vegetables" by Meish Goldish from THEMATIC POEMS, SONGS, AND FINGERPLAYS (Scholastic, 1993); used by permission of the publisher. "Puppy" from UP THE WINDY HILL by Aileen Fisher; copyright ©1953 by Abelard Press. © renewed by Aileen Fisher; reprinted by permission of Marian Reiner for the author. "Surprises" by Jean Conder Soule appeared originally in the RANDOM HOUSE BOOK OF POETRY FOR CHILDREN; attempts to reach the author have not been successful.

Art Permissions POPPY by Georgia O'Keeffe; gift of Charles C. and M. Stevenson Hender, Museum of Fine Arts, St. Petersburg, FL. VEGETABLES by Henri Matisse. STILL LIFE WITH THREE PUPPIES by Paul Gauguin; the Museum of Modern Art, New York, NY; Mrs. Simon Guggenheim Fund; photograph © 1997, the Museum of Modern Art, New York, NY. LA PIÑATA by Diego Rivera; courtesy of Hospital Infantil de Mexico Federico Gomez.

Photo credits pp. 12, 21, 26, 35, 40, 47, 52, 59: courtesy The Bettmann Archive. All remaining photographs courtesy of the author.

Cover design by Vincent Ceci and Jaime Lucero

Interior design by Ellen Matlach Hassell for Boultinghouse & Boultinghouse, Inc.

Interior Illustrations by Maxie Chambliss and Manuel Rivera

ISBN 0-590-92564-4

Copyright © 1996 by Rhonda Graff Silver. All rights reserved.

12 11 10 9 8 7 6 5 4 3 2 1   6 7 8 9/9/01/0

Contents

Introduction

I am not an artist, but I love learning about art. So, as a teacher, I decided it might be fun to share the world of art with my young students. That's how the art appreciation program described in this book came to be. It began as a kernel of an idea, a way to add sparkle to my first-grade curriculum. But this little notion soon grew into more than I ever imagined or could have hoped for.

I began by setting aside one full morning per week as a special time when my class of 25 children could learn about artists and discuss art reproductions. To prepare, I selected a favorite artist, focused on a theme or an artist, and began to look at books, posters, and postcards for reproductions. Materials assembled, I introduced the artist and the art and provided appropriate background information. The children responded naturally to the artwork as they saw it. My acceptance of their observations helped them realize that, when it comes to art appreciation, there are no right or wrong answers.

The art we explored inspired in-class art projects. By highlighting different features evident in each masterpiece, such as medium, theme, content or design, and by offering children the time and materials they needed to create collections of their own work, they were encouraged to appreciate the fine art while respecting their own ideas. In response to

the fine art, children painted on paper and canvas, drew with crayons and markers, dipped into watercolors, and created collages. As their knowledge increased, so did their desire to learn and see more. Their enthusiasm coaxed me to expand our art study.

An inviting learning center for studying art masterpieces

I began relying on language arts as a key component in our focus on art appreciation. I helped children develop art logs in which they tested new art-related vocabulary when recording their observations and feelings regarding art. In addition, we assembled individual and class books. At every opportunity possible, I integrated literature and poetry into our explorations. Our follow-up art activities soon touched other related areas of the curriculum, including math, science, and social studies. But (and I'm being honest here) as our art study gathered steam, the lines separating the disciplines tended to blur as one art-inspired activity led to another.

As the year came to an end, we celebrated by establishing a gallery showing at our local library. Children hosted the event, attended by families and friends, and proudly showed off their original creations. Looking back, I realize that the benefits of our art appreciation program are too numerous to count. I discovered that by devoting a solid block of time to doing something children love—namely art—it was easier and more exciting than ever to infuse my total curriculum with meaningful content children care about. Throughout the school year, I saw young children who never before encountered art masterpieces become eager to learn more. And their enthusiasm about art wasn't limited to the classroom. Parents told me their children begged to visit museums and were beginning to identify artists and their works when they saw them in homes and magazines. It pleases me to know my little experiment has helped my young students develop a new interest that can grow with them throughout their lives. As for me, I am more committed than ever to introducing students to artists and their art, and to looking for more ways to integrate art study across my curriculum. I hope this book helps you begin to do the same.

Rhonda Graff Silver

Rhonda Graff Silver

General Tips for an Artist Study

Choosing an Artist

An artist study is a flexible activity and you shouldn't be afraid to experiment. Consider choosing an artist or artwork related to personal interest, classroom themes, a specific time period, style, or subject matter. Allow students and their interests to help guide your plans. Gather reproductions wherever you can! (It is important to refer to the art as "reproductions" and explain to children the difference between "an original" and "a reproduction.")

Children working in small groups, looking at, discussing, and recording information about a postcard reproduction

Planning and Organizing

After signing on to the idea of including an art appreciation study in your class, you'll need to give a bit of thought to how you will organize and present the materials, as well as the class groupings for each activity. For example, you might want to introduce the art and start-up activities to the whole group of children, while placing the follow-up activities in learning centers. That way, children working cooperatively in small groups may encounter art experiences throughout the week.

Keep in mind, if young children are working on a full-scale, hands-on art project, that it's best to allow them a large block of time at least once a week to engage in the work. This way, children can work without feeling rushed, making observations and experimenting in a relaxed manner.

In any event, keep your activities child-centered and fun. Display reproductions, books about artists, biographical information, and students' artwork in the center or classroom. This book suggests numerous activities for you to use. Pick and choose those activities that work best for you and your students, and develop your own.

Tips and Activities for Enriching Art Exploration

◆ Have children keep art logs by providing notebooks where they can record their thoughts, feelings, and responses to the art they study. Invite children to personalize their logs with cover illustrations. Plan a mini-session so you can model how to write an entry on chart pad paper. Be ready to guide children's writing efforts with some open-ended questions: *What did you see? What did you like or dislike? What was interesting from the class discussion? Who is the artist? How did the art make you feel?* Encourage children to use temporary spelling and to accompany their work with illustrations.

◆ If possible, schedule a class trip to a museum or gallery. Even public libraries often display collections worth visiting. While at the library, inquire if they have a lending program that allows you to borrow art reproductions. Send away for catalogs from museum bookstores and catalogs featuring collections of poster art. Send home a note encouraging families to take their children to museums and galleries. Include a list of local spots they might consider, with the phone numbers so families can have easy access to necessary visitor information.

◆ Consider your school's art teacher a valuable resource. Invite him or her to your class to help students appreciate the art posters included in this book. Encourage the art teacher to bring in and share any related materials with the class.

◆ Take photographs of students working. Post them on a bulletin board and again at your gallery if you choose to have one. Have children dictate captions describing the processes they are engaged in. And most important, while children work, jot notes describing how they approach and respond to the activities presented. Which children enjoy tactile experiences? Which children prefer writing about art masterpieces to creating their own? Which children have an eye for color? By watching children engage in art activities, you can gain valuable insights into their interests and learning styles.

Art Log

Students working on still life creations

About This Book

This book is divided into four main parts. Each part is devoted to one of four artists: Georgia O'Keeffe, Henri Matisse, Paul Gauguin, and Diego Rivera. Each offers information and activities designed to help acquaint young students with that artist and his or her work, and includes the following components:

The author sharing reproductions with her students

Notes on the Masterpiece

This section provides general information about each reproduction. You might want to share these informative points with the class after the children have had a chance to make their own interpretations and observations.

Discussion Springboards

These prompts will help you introduce the art to the group. Remember that these are suggested warm-ups. If you have used art reproductions in your class, or if you feel comfortable experimenting, feel free to devise an introduction that works for you and your class.

Portrait of the Artist

This section provides detailed information that will help bring the artist to life. You might read the information aloud to children and then share the artist mini-book found in the Curriculum Connections section. A copy of each Portrait of the Artist section can also be mounted on construction paper and displayed alongside the poster reproduction of his or her work. Along the lower border of each Portrait of the Artist section you will find a time line highlighting the artist's life and accomplishments. Consider having children develop their own time lines throughout the school year.

Curriculum Connections

This section outlines activities designed to help you integrate each reproduction into the curriculum—language arts, math, science, social studies, geography, and art. Reproducible activities are included in each section. Keep in mind that it is not necessary to do all the activities presented. Choose a few favorites, or plan an expanded artist study by changing or augmenting the offerings to suit your needs.

The teaching assistant sharing reproductions from a book about Georgia O'Keeffe

More Ideas to Try

This section presents additional ideas to help round out your art appreciation study. It is also meant to help spark your own ideas. Suggestions for special activities such as scheduling trips or hosting guest speakers are included here.

Culminating Activity

This activity suggests a creative way to wrap up each artist study. There is one culminating activity for each artist, but they are fairly interchangeable. It's suggested that you read them all before deciding on any one. You may find yourself borrowing bits and pieces from each ending activity, thus customizing your own commencement celebration.

Book Breaks

This section features an annotated list of related children's literature so that you can more easily integrate literature into your art program. How you use the books and how they fit into your overall art appreciation program depends heavily on the content of each. One title may be related to the mood or theme of the art, while another may address issues involving art technique and color, or may feature a biography of an artist's life. It's best to have as many titles as you can assemble, so students can be treated to a variety of perspectives and can understand art study as a multifaceted adventure.

Poppy
by Georgia O'Keeffe

Poppy
1927,
oil on canvas,
30 x 36 inches

The masterpiece *Poppy,* by artist Georgia O'Keeffe, is the perfect choice for introducing young children to fine art. Children are easily intrigued by size, color, and elements of nature, and *Poppy* delivers all three. Use the following information and activities to bring O'Keeffe and her *Poppy* to life in your classroom.

NOTES ON THE MASTERPIECE

Georgia O'Keeffe painted many types of flowers. Her *Poppy* appears so big it spreads out to the edges of the canvas; there is no other object in the painting with which to make a size comparison. The brilliant petals are open so the viewer can see the inner part of the flower. The red is bright and powerful. In many of her paintings, O'Keeffe used color and shape to entice the viewer. The background might be a mountain or a cave—we'll never know for sure. (O'Keeffe didn't like it when people tried to explain her paintings because only she knew what her thoughts were and how her paintings came to be.) O'Keeffe enjoyed painting poppies and completed others—*Oriental Poppies* and *Red Poppy*. Her flower paintings were very popular.

Discussion Springboard

Display the poster with the reproduction of *Poppy*. Conceal the title of the art with sticky notes. Have children look at the reproduction and share their personal responses to the artwork. Encourage observations with open-ended questions such as:

- What do you see?
- Describe the flower.
- What colors do you see?
- What is in the middle of the picture? on the outside?
- Can you name any parts of the flower we don't see in this reproduction?
- Do you like or dislike this piece of art? Why?
- What is the setting of this painting; where do you think this flower is—inside? in a garden? outside? in the wild?
- What makes this flower look real?
- What makes this flower look artificial or pretend?
- Why do you think the artist, Georgia O'Keeffe, painted flowers?
- Why do you think she painted them to look so large?
- What do you think the name of this masterpiece might be?

Record all responses and observations on a large piece of chart pad paper. Add the actual title of the artwork to the top of the chart paper. Display the chart paper alongside the poster. Use highlighting marker to highlight key vocabulary words (for example, *flower, red, nature*). Encourage children to refer to the chart as they write in their art logs. Conclude this session by sharing with children any information you have gathered about this art masterpiece and related works.

Portrait of the Artist: GEORGIA O'KEEFFE

Georgia O'Keeffe, born November 15, 1887, on a farm in Wisconsin, was a great twentieth-century artist. As a young girl her artistic talents were evident, and she and her sisters were given art lessons. Even when she was young, Georgia O'Keeffe was very critical of her art. Still, she knew that she wanted to be an artist when she grew up. As a young adult, she studied at the Art Institute of Chicago, Art Students League of New York, and Teachers College, Columbia University. Later she taught art at a public school in Texas and at various colleges and universities throughout the United States.

Georgia O'Keeffe (1887–1986)

Georgia O'Keeffe liked to be alone when she painted. But, despite her reputation of being a loner, she was sociable and had close friends. She had two chow dogs that were very special to her. She usually wore simple black and white outfits.

1887	1905	1907	1914	1916	1917
Georgia O'Keeffe born, November 15, in Wisconsin	attended the Art Institute of Chicago	attended Art Students League of New York	attended Teachers College, Columbia University	first showing of her work at Stieglitz's gallery, 291	one-woman show, sold her first painting

O'Keeffe loved her library, where she wrote letters to friends and family. Her art was always her prime concern. She was easy-going and accepting, except when it came to herself and her art.

Georgia O'Keeffe didn't enjoy copying work or being told what was "right." Her art tools were like a language to her, allowing her to say what she wanted. In 1915, she began to develop her own style. Georgia O'Keeffe expressed her emotions, feelings, and reactions to things around her through her art. She told others that she found she could say things with color and shapes that she couldn't say in any other way—things she had no words for.

With the help of Alfred Stieglitz, a well-known photographer and owner of the New York gallery, 291, the public got its first look at Georgia O'Keeffe's work in 1916. In 1917, Stieglitz hosted O'Keeffe's first one-woman show at his gallery. This was special because O'Keeffe was an American-educated woman artist, and at this time most artists were European-educated men. In 1918, Georgia O'Keeffe gave up teaching art and moved to New York to begin her career as an artist. She and Stieglitz were married in 1924.

In 1929, Georgia O'Keeffe traveled to New Mexico, where she became interested in the desert, landscapes, rocks, and churches as well as flowers. In the early 1930s while in New Mexico she began her paintings of bones with flowers. In 1949 she made New Mexico her home.

In Georgia O'Keeffe's lifetime she painted more than two hundred flower pictures. She painted with feeling about the beauty of nature.

1924	1927	1930	1946	1949	1986
married Stieglitz	painted *Poppy*	traveled to New Mexico	Stieglitz died	moved to New Mexico permanently	Georgia O'Keeffe died

Curriculum Connections

✎ Mini-Book

(LANGUAGE ARTS/SOCIAL STUDIES)

Use reproducible page 21 to create a mini-biography booklet about Georgia O'Keeffe. Read the information to the children. Distribute copies of the booklets and help children fold their booklets along the dotted lines as shown in the diagram. Read the text through again, then invite children to add illustrations in the spaces provided. If you like, discuss the meanings of the words *real* and *abstract*. Suggest that children share their mini-books with family and friends.

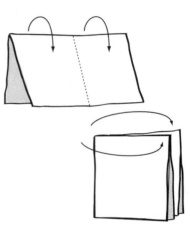

✎ Poetry Prompt

(LANGUAGE ARTS)

The poem "What Is Red?" can be used to help children focus on the many moods and shades of red that color their daily experiences. Before sharing the poem with the class, ask students to brainstorm what "red" means to them. List their responses on a large piece of chart pad paper. Then read the poem aloud. Read the poem again, this time asking children to close their eyes as they picture the imagery suggested. Ask children to tell if the poem helped them to think of any more items to add to their list. Then copy the poem (two lines to a page) onto large sheets of drawing paper and have children work individually or in pairs to illustrate the lines. Bind the illustrated lines in sequence into a book. Add red construction paper covers and the poem's title. Consider having children make similar books representing other colors by substituting new words for this poem (for example, "Yellow is butter, Sunny and bright...") and then illustrating these new lines.

🖌 Paint Chips (MATH/LANGUAGE ARTS)

Visit a home design center or a hardware store and select a number of paint chip samples (at least two of each) representing shades of red. Back in class, show the strips to children and read the names of the colors together. Cut individual chips apart (leaving color names on, if possible). Place these in a box and have children take turns matching and sorting the chips into pairs or by color hues ranging from darkest to lightest. As a related language arts activity designed to acquaint children with similes, you might have children each select a red chip and then provide drawing papers printed with the following sentence: This red paint chip (glue chip here) is as red as _____. Children can then illustrate their sentences and bind the finished pages into a class book.

🖌 Color Word Book (ART)

Color Word Book

Have children each label a piece of paper with two color words, for example, *red* and *blue*. Provide different materials of the chosen two colors, such as construction paper pieces, cellophane, watercolors, crayons, or tissue paper to decorate each page. Add as many pages featuring other color combinations as you wish. Add a last page labeled "Rainbow." Show children how to number their pages and help them to create a Table of Contents for their books. They may add a dedication page, too.

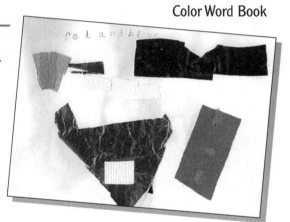

🖌 Venn Diagram (LANGUAGE ARTS/SCIENCE)

Copy the Venn diagram from Flower Comparison (reproducible page 22) onto chart paper and display. Also, make a photocopy for each child. Present two different real flowers or representations for children to observe. Choose from reproductions of Georgia O'Keeffe's flower art, samples of real flowers, and pictures or photos of flowers. Discuss the flowers with the children, having them describe what they know. Begin recording their observations on chart paper in the form of a Venn diagram. Identify the middle area of the Venn diagram as a place to record similarities and the outer areas as places for differences. Have children copy these recordings onto their own Venn diagrams. Supply extra copies of the reproducible so children can create their own Venn diagrams using different subject matter. For these independent efforts, children can use temporary spelling or drawings to show simi-

ROSE
thorns
grows
on bush

BOTH
flower
red

TULIP
grows
from a
bulb

larities and differences. For example, children might use a Venn diagram to compare and contrast *Poppy* to another work of art by Georgia O'Keeffe or to artwork by another artist.

Color Mixing (SCIENCE)

Distribute reproducible page 23 and let children use crayons, pastels, or paints to explore the color combination possibilities. Help them complete the information together based on their explorations. Ask: *What are the primary colors? What are the secondary colors? What will happen when all the colors are mixed together?*

> **Teaching Tip** Here are some basic principles of color mixing:
> * The primary colors are red, blue, and yellow.
> * The secondary colors are purple, orange, and green.
> * When any two primary colors are mixed together, a new color is made. These new colors are called secondary colors.
> * When the three primary colors are mixed together brown, black, or gray results.

Collaborative Flower Collage
(ART/MATH)

Provide groups of children with large pieces of pastel-colored poster board, some discarded magazines (women's, home decorating, animal, nature, and children's magazines work well), glue, and scissors. Invite the groups to flip through the magazines and clip out any individual flower pictures they see (the larger, the better). Help them glue the pictures collage-style (with edges overlapping) onto the poster board. To weave a bit of math into the activity, you can challenge children to collect a predetermined number of flowers. For example, you might ask children to include 100 flowers in their collage while asking them to figure out how many flowers they each need to contribute to such an array. For more of a challenge, ask children to assemble 100 flowers representing a predetermined number of colors (for instance, 25 red flowers, 25 yellow flowers, 25 white flowers, and 25 pink flowers). Or assemble your collage first, then record a math problem representing the color or type of flowers represented (for example, 15 daisies + 32 roses + 3 pansies + 10 sunflowers = 60 flowers).

🖌 Flower Parts (SCIENCE/LANGUAGE ARTS)

Georgia O'Keeffe wanted people to take time to see what she saw in flowers. Supply children with an assortment of flowers. Ask local florists to donate some flowers for school use. Let them know you will be dissecting them, because some flowers work better than others. Lilies and gladioluses are good flowers to dissect. Provide children with hand lenses to examine the flower parts. To begin, allow children to explore freely using their senses including sight, touch, smell, and hearing—but not taste! **Remind children NEVER to eat flowers because some are poisonous!** After children have had time to explore, look at a flower together as a class, dissect it, and discuss any observations or questions. Work together to identify the simple flower parts (leaves, petals, stem, and so on). Use tiny sticky notes to label parts of the flower and then display the dissected parts.

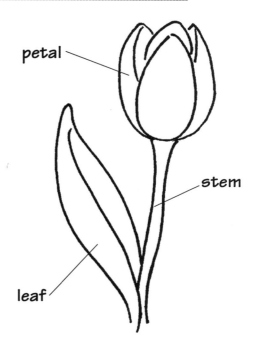

🖌 Flower Patterns (MATH)

Invite children to create their own flower-pattern pictures: red, red, purple, red, red, purple... tall, short, tall, short...with stem, without stem, without stem... Put the flower patterns on display. Have children identify the patterns created by their classmates. Children can also write log entries or number sentences describing how they constructed their flower patterns.

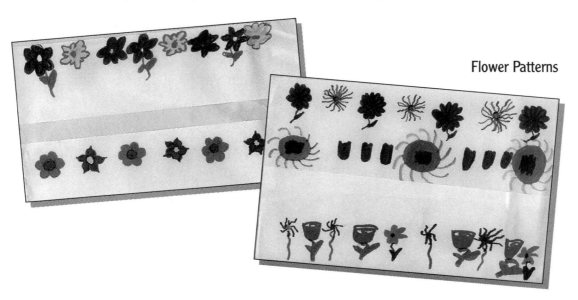

Flower Patterns

17

✎ Still Life Creations (ART)

Georgia O'Keeffe stretched the definition of still life with her *Poppy*. Note how O'Keeffe made her poppy so big. Introduce the term *still life* and help children to understand it as a picture of inanimate objects: flowers, vases, fruit.

You Will Need:

assorted objects to create a still life setting (table, cloth, bowls, vases, fruit) ❀ flowers (real, silk, dried) ❀ drawing paper ❀ crayons and markers ❀ paints and brushes ❀ pastels (optional)

Steps:

1. Choose objects from around the classroom to include in a still life. You may need to bring in a few objects from home, including flowers (real or artificial). Ask children to supplement the still life setup with objects of their own liking. Remind them not to bring in anything that is breakable or valuable. (If a glass vase is used, be sure to inform the class and discuss glass safety issues.)

2. Set up a *simple* scene by choosing interesting objects and arranging them in a pleasing way. Have children work in small groups to experiment with attractive setups.

3. Distribute art supplies and have children take turns interpreting the same still life using a variety of techniques (sketches, paintings, and so on).

4. Hang the finished art near the still life display.

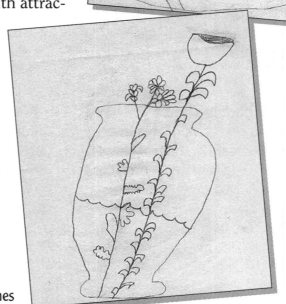

Still life sketches

More Ideas to Try

🌸 Acquaint children with local flower varieties. Have children plant and grow flowers in gardens indoors or out. Graph children's favorites.

🌸 Press some favorite flower varieties and create a class book. Dry others and use them to create gifts from nature.

🌸 Take a nature walk. Have children tote sketchpads along so they can pause and sketch observations.

🌸 Arrange for a trip to a local florist. Have children prepare a list of questions to pose to the florist.

Culminating Activity

Appreciation Day displays

Plan an Art Appreciation Day in which you invite other classes to share in the art you've come to know so well. Discuss the objective of this event with children. Have children decorate T-shirts or hats to make the day more festive! Serve dishes related to the artist you are celebrating—for Georgia O'Keeffe, for example, flower-shaped cookies and red fruit punch add a festive touch. Display the poster art and have volunteers share their related journal entries. Engage students' help in becoming tour guides and explaining the fine points of the fine art to their schoolmates. This is a time for children to share their work and knowledge — they should be proud of their accomplishments.

Book Breaks

- *Georgia O'Keeffe: Getting to Know the World's Greatest Artists* by Mike Venezia (Children's Press, 1993). This informative, fun biography helps introduce young children to the life and art of Georgia O'Keeffe.

- *The Reason for a Flower* by Ruth Heller (Grosset & Dunlap, 1983). Using these beautiful illustrations and informative text we can learn about pollination, seeds, flowers, flower parts, herbivores, and carnivores.

- *Hailstones and Halibut Bones: Adventures in Color* by Mary O'Neill and John Wallner (Doubleday, 1990). This selection of color poems enables children to experience each color in a unique way.

- *Alison's Zinnia* by Anita Lobel (Greenwillow Books, 1990). This alphabet book highlights one flower for each letter. A beautiful illustration and a letter appropriate flower sentence make up each page.

Still life creations

- *Planting a Rainbow* by Lois Ehlert (Harcourt Brace Jovanovich, 1988). A flower garden comes to life as a child and mother plant a rainbow of flowers. The colors are emphasized as the flowers bloom.

- *The Flower Alphabet Book* by Jerry Pallotta and Leslie Evans (Charlesbridge, 1989). An alphabet book with tidbits of information about each flower. The illustrations are colorful and fun.

- *The Red Poppy* by Irmgard Lucht (Hyperion, 1995). A beautiful story about the life of a red poppy with informative details about poppies, flower parts, insects, and animals. The Author's Note shows how science and art come together to create this book.

- *The Tiny Seed* by Eric Carle (Simon and Schuster, 1991). Follow a tiny seed as it survives the perils of nature and the environment, traveling through the seasons to become a beautiful flower.

- *The Empty Pot* by Demi (Henry Holt, 1990). This story teaches a lesson about honesty as an emperor looks for the successor to his throne. All the children are given flower seeds with hopes of presenting the emperor with the best flowers. The winner would be emperor, but there is a twist....

Sometimes Georgia O'Keeffe's flowers looked real. Sometimes they looked abstract. But they always looked beautiful!

abstract   real

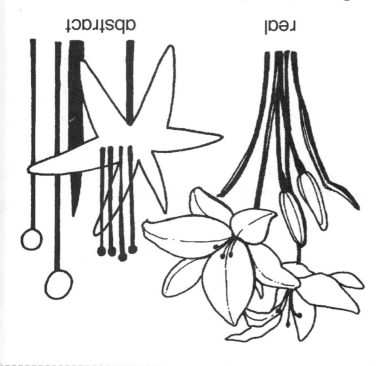

Georgia O'Keeffe created more than two hundred flower paintings in her lifetime. Red poppies, jack-in-the-pulpits, orchids, and lilies are some of the flowers she painted.

Fill this frame with flowers. They can look real or abstract.

Now you're an artist just like Georgia O'Keeffe!

Georgia O'Keeffe
(1887–1986)

Georgia O'Keeffe was a famous artist. She enjoyed nature. She painted pictures of flowers, rocks, mountains, and shells.

Name _____

Flower Comparison

Label the Venn diagram. What things are the same? Write them in the middle. What things are different? Write them on the outside parts of the circles under the correct label.

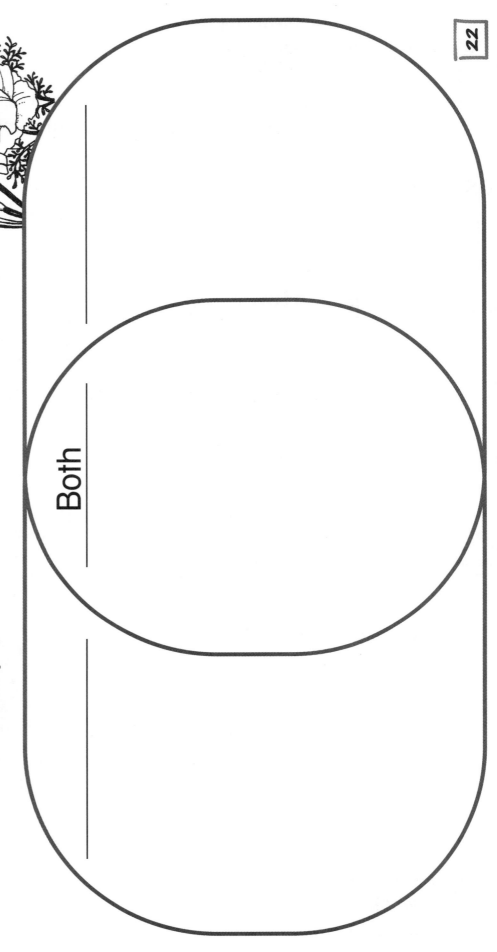

Both

Name _____

Create Colors!

Many of Georgia O'Keeffe's paintings were very colorful. Try the experiment below. First write your prediction. Then complete the experiment by mixing the colors in the box to the right. Write the color you get below your prediction.

I think red + blue = _____ .

red + blue =

I think blue + yellow = _____ .

blue + yellow =

I think yellow + red = _____ .

yellow + red =

I think red + blue + yellow = _____ .

red + blue + yellow =

Turn the paper over. Try mixing your own colors. What colors can you make?

Vegetables by Henri Matisse

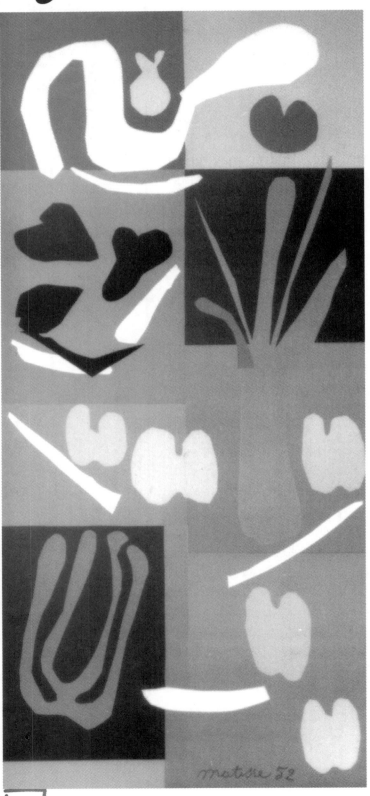

matisse 52

Vegetables
1951, gouache on paper, 69 x 31⅞ inches

F inally! Some good-for-you vegetables children will love to sample! *Vegetables,* a paper cut-out design by Henri Matisse, features an amusing assortment of veggies splayed against a delightful color-block background. Regard it as a whimsical way to help children explore colors, shapes, and design. And be prepared to serve up more than one helping of the *Vegetables*-inspired activities described on the following pages.

NOTES ON THE MASTERPIECE

Vegetables is an example of a Matisse paper cut-out. It was created in 1951 and signed in 1952. It is made from paper painted with gouache (pronounced gwäsh), an opaque watercolor. The paper was painted, cut, and then pasted. He completed another paper cut, *Snow Flowers,* that some believe to be a matching piece, as it was completed the same year and had the same dimensions. The background of *Vegetables* is grid-like and simple. The images appear flat; each image seems to have its own section. Color is also highlighted because the sections of each color are big and clear. His cut-outs, like many of his paintings, were considered decorative works of art.

Discussion Springboard

Display the poster with the reproduction of *Vegetables*. Conceal the title of the art with sticky notes. Have children look at the reproduction and share their personal responses to the artwork. Encourage observations with open-ended questions such as:

- What do you see?

- Do you see anything that looks familiar? Describe it.

   (Although the vegetables are not realistic, children may report seeing peppers, celery, onion, broccoli, eggplants, and carrots. Encourage all responses and have children point to the vegetables they are identifying.)

- What colors do you see?

- What color stands out the most? Explain why you think this is so.

- What shapes do you see?

- How many objects can you count in this work of art?

- How does this artwork make you feel?

- What do you think the white shapes are supposed to be?

- What do you think the name of this masterpiece might be?

Record all responses and observations on a large piece of chart pad paper. Add the title of the artwork to the top of the chart paper. Display the chart paper alongside the poster. Use highlighting marker or tape to highlight key vocabulary words (for example, *peppers, shapes, yellow*). Encourage children to refer to it as they keep their art logs. Conclude this session by sharing with children any information you have gathered about this art masterpiece and related works.

Portrait of the Artist: HENRI MATISSE

Henri Matisse was born at his grandparents' home in Le Cateau-Cambresis in the north of France in 1869. To please his father, Matisse began to study law, but he soon realized the power painting had for him. By 1891, Matisse decided to give up law and pursue life as an artist.

Matisse spent time at the Louvre, a museum in Paris, viewing and copying art in order to study the masters' techniques and learn more about painting. He gave credit to the masters for all that he had accomplished. In the 1890s, he became interested in modern art and his works began to change, becoming softer and brighter. In 1905, Matisse became part of the group of controversial painters known as *les fauves*, which means "wild beasts." Their different-looking paintings were flat and very colorful, with swirls, splashes of color, and strong outlines.

Henri Matisse (1869–1954)

1869
Henri Matisse born, December 31, in the north of France

1891
began his career as an artist

1898
began work using bright, bold colors

1905
first fauve paintings

1937
designed scenery and costumes for a ballet

By the 1930s, Matisse's work was becoming known around the world. Using color as the focus of his art, Matisse painted still lifes, landscapes, and figures. He also became interested in decorative art. He collected fabrics from around the world and used them in his decorative paintings. Nature also influenced Matisse's work.

In the 1940s, Matisse became ill and was forced to stay in bed or a wheelchair for most of the day. While he was in bed, he began using a long pole with charcoal on the end that enabled him to draw on the walls. In 1948, Matisse designed stained glass windows, ceramic murals, and the furniture for a chapel in Vence, France. Also during this era he began his famous paper cut-outs with flat, pure, vibrant colors. He learned to cut paper shapes and use his walls as canvases. Assistants moved and pinned the papers for him until he felt the composition was right. Then, when complete, the paper cut-outs were placed on another spot on the wall or pasted together. His book, *Jazz*, is a collection of such cut-outs. He also wrote the text in his own handwriting. The type is art itself—all different styles and sizes balancing the page.

In November 1954, Henri Matisse died while in Nice. But his art continues to bring happiness to those who view his masterpieces.

1940
health began to fail

1943
created paper cut-outs

1947
his book, *Jazz*, was published

1948
worked on designs for the chapel at Vence

1950
created more and more paper cut-outs

1951
created the paper cut-out *Vegetables*

1954
Henri Matisse died

Curriculum Connections

Mini-Book (LANGUAGE ARTS/SOCIAL STUDIES)

Use reproducible page 35 to create a mini-biography booklet about Henri Matisse. Read the information to children. Distribute copies of the booklets and help children fold their booklets along the dotted lines as shown in the diagram. Read the text through again, then invite children to add illustrations in the spaces provided. Suggest that children share their mini-books with family and friends.

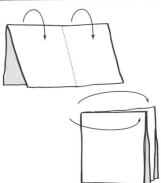

Poetry Prompt (LANGUAGE ARTS/SCIENCE)

Vegetables

Eat your vegetables,
Clean your plate!
Eat your vegetables,
Veggies are great!
String beans, broccoli,
Lettuce and peas,
Squash and brussels sprouts,
More corn, please!
Cucumbers, eggplant,
Beets and tomatoes,
Celery, carrots,
Spinach and potatoes.
Radishes, cauliflower,
Cabbage and cress,
Peppers and onions,
Asparagus? Yes!
Black beans, lima beans,
Soybeans, too.
Eat your veggies,
They're good for you!

—*Meish Goldish*

The poem "Vegetables" can be used to help children note the many vegetable varieties available to them. Before sharing the poem with the class, ask students to brainstorm a list of vegetables they know. List their responses on a large piece of chart pad paper. (Be prepared for some children to confuse fruits and vegetables and make a mental note to address this confusion.) Then read the poem aloud. Read the poem again, this time asking children to close their eyes as they picture the imagery suggested. Ask children to tell if the poem helped them to think of any more items to add to their list. Consider following up the poem with a veggie taste-testing fest. You might send notes home asking families to each contribute a different fresh vegetable variety for children to nibble on in class, while you provide some interesting dips (which tend to transform most veggies into a kid-friendly treat). Or you might bring in some unusual vegetable varieties for children to guess and/or sample. Still another activity idea is to bring in fresh, frozen and canned versions of the same vegetable variety (corn and carrots work well for this) and compare and contrast the color, shape, texture, and taste of the three different types. **(When sampling foods, always be aware of possible food allergies.)**

Color Count (MATH)

Matisse created many paper cut-outs. *Vegetables* is a fine example of this style of art. Display *Vegetables*. Create a chart to post information based on the reproduction. Children can create their own charts as well. Ask the questions below, inserting in the parentheses each color: yellow, blue, white, green.

- How many (yellow) shapes are there?

- What do you think the (yellow) shapes are?

- Are all the (yellow) shapes the same thing? Explain your observations.

- What other foods are (yellow)?

- What about the other colors in *Vegetables*? What do you think they are? Do you think they might be food?

Encourage children to ask each other similar questions when they create their own paper cut-outs (see page 31).

Graph-a-Veggie (MATH)

You Will Need: assortment of real vegetables (radishes, carrots, potatoes, green beans) plastic graphing mat reproducible pages 36 and 37

Steps:

1. Bring in an assortment of real vegetables or have each child bring in a specified vegetable. Gather children in a group to make a "real object" graph in which the actual object represents itself.

2. Use a table or the floor to sort and count the vegetables according to variety.

3. Place the vegetables on a large plastic graphing mat if available (or make one on a plastic garbage bag or shower curtain with a masking tape grid).

4. Once the vegetables are arranged, ask children to discuss the graph results.

5. Distribute the pictograph on page 36. Using the real-objects graph as a reference, have each student draw pictures of vegetables on the paper graph. If there are four real radishes on the real-objects graph, children should draw four radishes, one in each box, on their paper graphs.

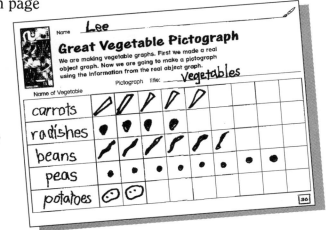

6. Children should continue drawing all the vegetables that correspond with the number of real vegetables. Children can also color the vegetables.

EXTENSION Children can create bar graphs on reproducible page 37 by coloring in one square on each grid for each vegetable located on the real-objects graph. Bar graphs can be color-coded to match the color of the vegetables.

Vegetable Print Patterns

(MATH/ART)

Matisse's paper cut-out *Vegetables* features a variety of vegetables that he cut out from his collection of papers. They appear as assorted shapes.

You Will Need: assorted vegetables ✄ knife (adult use only) • water-based paint ✄ sponges or paper towels ✄ newspaper ✄ paper

Steps:

1. Cut the vegetables in half (or slice or dice into smaller sections).

2. Pour a bit of paint onto a sponge or a few folded layers of paper toweling placed on newspaper. Prepare different colors for children to dip into.

3. Have children dip cut sides of the vegetables into the paint and press firmly onto a piece of paper.

4. When children feel comfortable printing, have them create patterns using the vegetable prints. Have children describe each other's patterns.

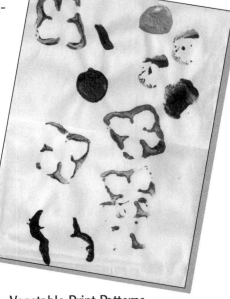

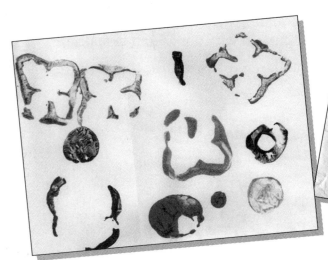

Vegetable Print Patterns

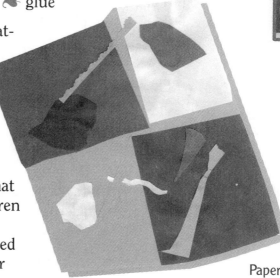

✏️ Paper Cut-outs (ART)

You Will Need: assortment of brightly colored paper (including vibrant neon colors, if possible) 🍃 scissors 🍃 glue

Have children think of a favorite subject matter to inspire their own paper cut-outs. (You might want to precut the colored papers into smaller sizes so that children can manipulate the paper more easily.) Have children experiment with composition by selecting a contrasting background paper and then pushing their loose paper cut-outs around this way and that against the background paper. Inform children that Matisse made many changes before he liked what he saw. When children are satisfied with their arrangements, they can glue their shapes in place.

Paper Cut-outs

✏️ Fabric Fun (ART)

Matisse collected fabrics from around the world, which he used on tables, walls, and floors in his paintings. They were decorative and colorful with beautiful patterns and designs that added to his work. Have children create a decorative composition using fabrics. They can create a picture or a collage. The main idea is for children to look at the way the colors and patterns work together.

You Will Need: fabric swatches 🍃 glue 🍃 scissors 🍃 tagboard or construction paper in assorted sizes

Steps:

1. Place fabric swatches in baskets or tins for the children to examine and choose from. Provide scissors and glue.

> **Teaching Tip**
> To obtain a variety of fabrics, ask parents to send in fabric scraps. Also check local fabric stores for post-holiday sales on seasonal fabric.

Children choosing fabrics

2. Distribute tagboard to each student (or student pairs). Determine what size paper you want children to use or let them decide.

3. Have children decorate the paper using the fabrics in any way they choose.

4. Display the finished collages.

Fabric Fun

Foreground/Background (ART)

Matisse is known for his use of vibrant color. What happens when two colors are next to each other? Do the colors affect each other? What color shirt looks good on you? What colors look good together? Create some color cut-outs to see how colors work. This can be done as a class demonstration with assistance from children, or each child can experiment on his or her own.

You Will Need: assortment of solid-colored paper or fabrics, cut to 4-inch-by-6-inch rectangles ❦ scissors ❦ glue ❦ large sheets of paper or tagboard

Steps:

1. Provide an assortment of solid colored papers or precut fabric rectangles to use for both shape cut-outs and background colors.

2. Choose a shape or shapes and cut out the exact shape(s) six times from the same color paper.

> **Teaching Tip**
> To get multiples of the same shape and to speed cutting, stack the precut rectangles on top of each other.

3. Have each student choose six different uncut pieces to serve as backgrounds on which to glue the shapes from step 2. Glue these, with edges touching, to an uncut piece of construction paper or tagboard. Trim edges of the uncut piece to match outer edges of cut pieces, if desired.

4. Have students glue one shape piece to each of the background pieces. Ask: *How does the shape appear on the different colors? Do the different backgrounds change how the shape appears?* Discuss your observations.

> **Teaching Tip**
> Students can record observations in their art logs.

Foreground/Background art

 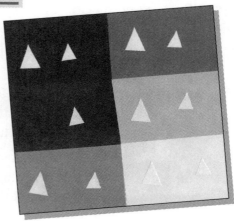

More Ideas to Try

🌿 Matisse played the violin. Read *I See a Song* by Eric Carle. The book has assorted colorful collages done in typical Eric Carle style. Have children share their thoughts about the pictures in response to the opening statement presented in this otherwise wordless book.

🌿 Using the paper cut-out *Vegetables*, discuss the four food groups and digestion.

🌿 Matisse wanted his art to make people comfortable and happy. Use magazines, newspapers, and photos to create a "Happy Collage."

🌿 Invite an interior decorator to visit the class and discuss use of color and fabrics.

Culminating Activity

Using an assortment of fabrics, create a class quilt. Have children stitch or glue individual quilt squares to a bedsheet. Meanwhile, sew a length of fiberfill to a same-size sheet to create a quilt backing. Glue or stitch the quilt top to the prepared backing. For a simpler quilt, children can use fabric crayons to draw pictures on squares of paper and then an adult can transfer the designs to a quilt top (sheet) with a hot iron. Filling and backing may be sewn on later by machine, or the "quilt" panel may simply be hung without backing from a ceiling wire to serve as a decorative room divider.

Book Breaks

- *Meet Matisse* by Nelly Munthe (Little, Brown, 1983). This book for children introduces Matisse's paper cut-outs. Included are some related art projects to try.

- *I See a Song* by Eric Carle (Scholastic, 1996). This book has only one page of text, which invites the reader to imagine and feel all that music, art, and color can evoke. The rest of the book is full of illustrations that are colorful and fun.

- *Jazz* by Henri Matisse (George Braziller, 1983). This collection of Matisse paper cut-outs, with text by the artist, gives a personal perspective. The text is not background for the cut-outs. The introduction tells about the making of the book.

- *Color* by Ruth Heller (Putnam & Grosset, 1995). Beautifully illustrated and vibrantly colored, this book written in rhyme explains the printing process, color mixing, and use of color.

- *Mouse Paint* by Ellen Stoll Walsh (Harcourt Brace Jovanovich, 1989). Following the adventures of three mice and a cat, children learn what happens when colors are mixed.

- *Lunch* by Denise Fleming (Henry Holt, 1992). A little mouse enjoys an assortment of vegetables and fruits as it eats its way through lunch and gets ready for dinner. Great examples of adjectives, too!

- *Growing Vegetable Soup* by Lois Ehlert (Harcourt Brace Jovanovich, 1990). A child and father decide to make vegetable soup. Starting with planting, and ending with eating, we see how to grow vegetables and make soup.

- *Color Dance* by Ann Jonas (Greenwillow, 1989). Color mixing is shown as three girls dance with colorful scarves.

- *The Keeping Quilt* by Patricia Polacco (Simon and Schuster, 1988). A family comes to the U.S. from Russia, and a very special quilt is made using fabrics from family possessions. The quilt is handed down from generation to generation...and treasured every step of the way. Note the use of fabrics.

Using his scissors, Henri Matisse cut shapes from painted paper. He created many beautiful works of art. **Vegetables** is an example of a paper cut-out.

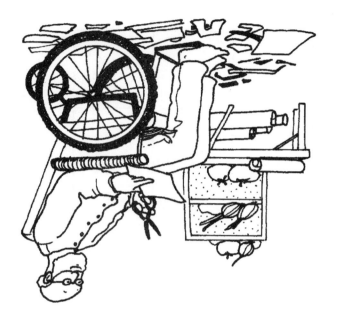

Henri Matisse loved to use bright colors in his artwork. Color these objects with bright colors.

Matisse wanted his art to make people happy. Draw a picture of you doing something that makes you happy.

Henri Matisse
(1869–1954)

Henri Matisse was a talented artist. He painted, sculpted, and made book illustrations and paper cut-outs.

Name _____

Great Vegetable Pictograph

We are making vegetable graphs. First we made a real-objects graph. Now we are going to make a pictograph using the information from the real-objects graph.

Pictograph title: _____

Name of Vegetable				

Name _____

Great Vegetable Bar Graph

Color the boxes below to make a vegetable bar graph.
Use the information from your pictograph.

Bar graph title: _____

Name of Vegetable

Still Life With Three Puppies by Paul Gauguin

Still Life With Three Puppies
1888, oil on wood,
36⅛ x 24⅝ inches

Paul Gauguin's masterpiece *Still Life With Three Puppies* is brimming with the type of patterns and symbols children relish discovering. After all, what child could resist three squirmy puppies and a collection of odd-looking treats coupled with three mysterious-looking goblets filled with... well, who knows what? This is one masterpiece ripe with intrigue. Students will want to dig right in.

NOTES ON THE MASTERPIECE

In 1888 Gauguin painted *Still Life With Three Puppies*. The main subjects are the three puppies among other groups of three. There are three goblets with three "apples." Gauguin used thick outlines around his vividly colored subjects. This painting resembles Japanese art, which Gauguin admired. There is no perspective; this painting appears flat. It is located in the Museum of Modern Art in New York City.

Discussion Springboard

Display the poster with the reproduction of *Still Life With Three Puppies*. Conceal the title of the art with sticky notes. Have children look at the reproduction and share their personal responses to the artwork. Encourage observations with open-ended questions such as:

- What do you see?
- What are the animals doing?
- What is at the bottom of the picture?
- Do the animals look real? Explain why or why not.
- What do you think they are drinking?
- What do you think the three glasses are for?
- What do you think is in the glasses?
- Look at the background. What do you see?
- Where do you think this painting takes place?
- What colors do you see?
- Do the things in this painting look real?
- What do you think the name of this masterpiece might be?

Record all responses and observations on a large piece of chart pad paper. Add the actual title of the artwork to the top of the chart paper. Display the chart paper alongside the poster. Use highlighting marker or tape to highlight key vocabulary words (for example, *outlines, puppies, three*). Encourage children to refer to it as they write in their art logs. Conclude this session by sharing with children any information you have gathered about this art masterpiece and related works.

Portrait of the Artist: PAUL GAUGUIN

Paul Gauguin (1848–1903)

Paul Gauguin was born in 1848 in Paris. He began his career as an artist late in life. He is known for his painting, drawing, sculpture, and ceramics.

In 1849, Gauguin's family moved from Paris to Lima, Peru. In 1855, he returned to France to attend school, where he had difficulty making friends and getting along with others. Later, he enlisted in the Merchant Marine and the Navy. While he was away, his mother died, a tragedy that affected him deeply. Fortunately, she appointed a guardian, Gustave Arosa, a wealthy businessman and patron of the arts, who played an influential role in Gauguin's life. Arosa found him a job as a stockbroker.

In 1873, Gauguin married a Danish woman, Mette Gad, and they had five children. He became friendly with artists such as Camille Pissaro, an Impressionist painter. In April 1881, at the sixth Impressionist Exhibition, Gauguin's work was recognized.

1848	1849	1855	1865	1871	1873
Paul Gauguin born, June 7, in Paris	moved with family to Lima, Peru	moved back to France to attend school	assigned to a cargo ship after enlisting in Merchant Marine	began work as a stockbroker	married Mette Gad

In 1882, the stock market crashed and Gauguin decided to devote his life to art. But he was not successful selling his art. In 1886 Gauguin settled in Pont-Aven, among other artists who didn't like him but who respected his art. In 1887, he went to Panama, eventually working to dig the Panama Canal. He used the money earned to go to Martinique, an island that reminded him of the tropical world of his childhood.

Gauguin believed in the emotional power of line, color, and shape. His paintings were symbolic instead of realistic. Using line and vivid colors, Gauguin was freed from copying reality.

Between 1888 and 1891, Gauguin stayed with Vincent van Gogh in Arles, France. In 1891, on a trip funded by the French government, he set sail for Papeete, Tahiti. He settled in Mataiea, where the people lived in huts and houses surrounded by palm trees and beautiful water. He drew everyday life and figure studies, and let his imagination influence his work. Many people weren't used to Gauguin's art, which was filled with unusual, bright colors and different subjects from Tahiti. But working in a Paris studio, Gauguin gathered with other artists to discuss art, sing songs, and share ideas. He wrote a book called *Noa Noa* (meaning "fragrant" in Tahitian) that explained the paintings he did in Tahiti. He completed ten woodcuts to illustrate the book. Gauguin returned to Tahiti in 1895 but began to endure ups and downs, physically, mentally, and artistically.

Paul Gauguin died in May 1903. He lived most of his life alone, struggling to succeed as an artist. After his death, his work continued to grow in popularity and influenced many other artists who followed. Today, he is considered a leader of modern art.

1883 devoted life to becoming an artist

1886 moved to Brittany to the village of Pont-Aven

1888 painted *Still Life With Three Puppies*

1891 went to Tahiti

1901 moved to Marquesas Islands

1903 Paul Gauguin died

Curriculum Connections

 **Mini-Book** (LANGUAGE ARTS/SOCIAL STUDIES)

Use reproducible page 47 to create a mini-biography booklet about Paul Gauguin. Read the information to children. Distribute copies of the booklets and help children fold their booklets along the dotted lines as shown in the diagram. Read the text through again, then invite children to add illustrations in the spaces provided. Suggest that children share their mini-books with family and friends.

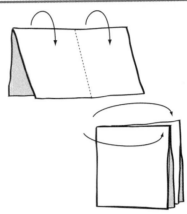

 Poetry Prompt (LANGUAGE ARTS/MATH)

My Puppy

It's funny
my puppy
knows just how I feel.

When I'm happy
he's yappy
and squirms like an eel.

When I'm grumpy
he's slumpy
and stays at my heel.

It's funny
my puppy
knows such a great deal.

—*Aileen Fisher*

The poem "My Puppy" can be used to help children focus on their experiences with puppy dogs and other pets. Before sharing the poem with the class, ask students to tell what they know about puppies, their needs, and behaviors. List their responses on a large piece of chart pad paper. Then read the poem aloud. Read the poem again, this time asking children to close their eyes as they picture the imagery suggested. Ask children to tell if the poem helped them to think of any more items to add to their list. Expand your discussion to include pets of any kind. Especially encourage children to share stories of how their pets affect their moods. Consider creating a class graph of favorite pets.

Triple Play (ART/MATH)

Gauguin's painting *Still Life With Three Puppies* features some objects that appear to be grouped in threes. There are three puppies, three goblets, and three "apples." Often in fairy tales and nursery rhymes, the number three is used to designate characters, wishes, animals, or magical charms. After looking at Gauguin's artwork and noting the use of three, read some fairy tales or nursery rhymes to children. Let them note all the uses of three. Using reproducible page 48, have children create a Triple Play Cube. Start by decorating the sides with images from Paul Gauguin's *Still Life With Three Puppies*, or images from a fairy tale or nursery rhyme featuring three elements. When completely decorated, have children cut out on the solid black outline and make creases on the dashed lines. Fold the paper into a cube and tape it together. Then display the Triple Play Cubes for all to see.

Teaching Tip
Here are some fairy tales and nursery rhymes that include three:
- Rumpelstiltskin
- Goldilocks and the Three Bears
- The Three Little Pigs
- Three Billy Goats Gruff
- Three Little Kittens
- Rub a Dub Dub, Three Men in a Tub

One, Two, Three...Skip-Count!

(MATH)

Use reproducible page 49 to introduce children to skip counting. Begin by counting by ones. Then tell them that skip counting is counting, but not using every number. For instance, if we count by twos we are counting every second number. If we count by threes we are counting every third number. Have children color in every other box in the first problem. By reading the numbers under the colored boxes, they can count by two. Have them write the numbers on the lines under the number boxes and have the class skip-count aloud by two. Then have them try skip counting by three by coloring the boxes above the numbers in the second problem, reading the numbers, and writing the numbers on the lines below.

Island Paradise (SOCIAL STUDIES/GEOGRAPHY)

Gauguin spent years living on the island of Tahiti. Many of his works are about Tahitian life and the people there. Life in Tahiti was different from life in Paris, despite that fact that Tahiti had become a French colony, and European ways were beginning to affect life on the island. Help children locate Tahiti on a map and let them see how small it is, though, in fact, it's the largest island in French Polynesia. Define an island as a piece of land that is surrounded com-

pletely by water. What water is completely surrounding Tahiti? *(South Pacific Ocean)*

- Gauguin spent the last part of his life in the Marquesas Islands located near Tahiti. Look for other islands on the map. Create a list of islands and identify the body of water that surrounds the piece of land.

- Gauguin also traveled to Panama and Martinique. Which one is an island? Locate them on a map. Would you like to live on an island? Explain the benefits and the disadvantages. Have you ever traveled to an island?

- Gauguin moved to Peru when he was a young boy. Locate Peru. Peru is located near the equator. What is the equator? What type of weather do you think they have in Peru? The areas near the equator are called the tropics. The weather in the tropics is usually hot.

Puppy Puppet Play (ART)

You Will Need: one 5-inch tagboard square for each puppet ⟡ markers, crayons, or colored pencils ⟡ glue ⟡ google eyes, felt balls, fake fur, and fabric scraps (optional) ⟡ one 1-inch-by-6-inch finger band for each puppet

Steps:

1. Have children draw a puppy face or full body on a precut square and cut it out. Encourage them to decorate the puppy simply with crayons or, if available, more elaborately with google eyes, felt ball noses, and fur.

2. Roll the finger bands and size them correctly to each child's finger with a piece of tape.

3. Attach the finished puppet to the finger band with tape, glue, or a staple.

4. Have children use their puppets to:

Puppy puppets

- perform a skit teaching others how to act around unknown dogs.

- perform a puppy show to explain pet owner responsibilities. Have the puppy puppets try to sell themselves to a family looking for a puppy. Why should someone adopt them? Act out a skit.

- perform a skit about an important safety issue such as bike safety or stranger safety.

🖌 More Ideas to Try

🐾 In Tahiti, Gauguin lived in a hut. Discuss different types of homes. Would climate have anything to do with the type of homes people have? What type of home do you live in?

🐾 Gauguin lived in Tahiti and painted life as he saw it. Learn more about Tahiti and the Pacific Ocean by doing research as a class. Try using some of Gauguin's other paintings to understand what he saw and how he lived.

🐾 Gauguin's *Still Life With Three Puppies* has some items that are grouped by threes. Try setting up a still life with items grouped by another number. Have children guess what the number is. Then have them interpret and draw the still life.

🐾 Allow children to take turns bringing pets for a visit.

Invitation for Gallery Opening

Culminating Activity

Locate a space (school or local library, cafeteria, class-room) to create a gallery displaying students' work. There are different options for displaying the children's work—bulletin boards, tables, showcases, and so on.

Display their original artwork, reproductions of work done by artists you have studied, related literature, student writing, and personal responses to the art. Include the class brainstorming charts for each reproduction and any group poems or center projects that were made. Mount each piece of two-dimensional artwork on construction paper to give it a finished look. Remind children to sign and title their work. Print explanation cards to label and clarify what was done. Have children create invitations and invite their families, friends, teachers, school personnel, and principal to your gala Gallery Opening.

A gallery display

Book Breaks

🐾 *Gauguin: Eyewitness Art* by Michael Howard (Dorling Kindersley, 1992). This nonfiction book provides information about Gauguin's life, including many colorful illustrations and facts.

🐾 *My Puppy Is Born* by Joanna Cole and Margaret Miller (William Morrow, 1991). Using photographs, this book shows the stages a puppy goes through, beginning with its mother's pregnancy, delivery, and the first eight weeks of life. A young girl adopts the puppy.

🐾 *Colors: A First Discovery Book* by Gallimard Jeunesse and Pascale de Bourgoing (Scholastic, 1991). The colorful overlays make this book a fun way to introduce color mixing to young children.

🐾 *Spot a Dog: Child's Book of Art* by Lucy Micklethwait (Dorling Kindersley, 1995). By viewing reproductions of famous artwork, the reader locates the dog in each of the thirteen paintings. A variety of styles and artists are presented. A fun, interactive book.

🐾 *Island Boy* by Barbara Cooney (Viking Penguin, 1988). Follow the youngest boy of a large family until his death as a grandfather, as he shows his love for the island on which he was raised.

🐾 *The First Dog* by Jan Brett (Harcourt Brace Jovanovich, 1988). Beautifully illustrated, this book tells about the relationship between boy and dog, as the dog's keen senses help protect the young boy.

Paul Gauguin used colors in new ways. If he felt something should be blue, he made it blue. Color this scene with different colors, like Gauguin did.

When he was 43 years old, Paul Gauguin moved to the island of Tahiti. He wanted to live a simple life on a beautiful tropical island.

Paul Gauguin painted people, landscapes, and objects from his everyday life. In the frame below, draw three objects that are a part of your everyday life.

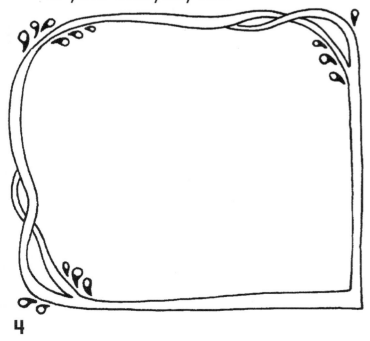

Paul Gauguin
(1848–1903)

Paul Gauguin was a French-born artist. Life as an artist was hard, but he kept painting. Paul Gauguin loved to paint!

Name _____

Triple Play Cube

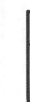

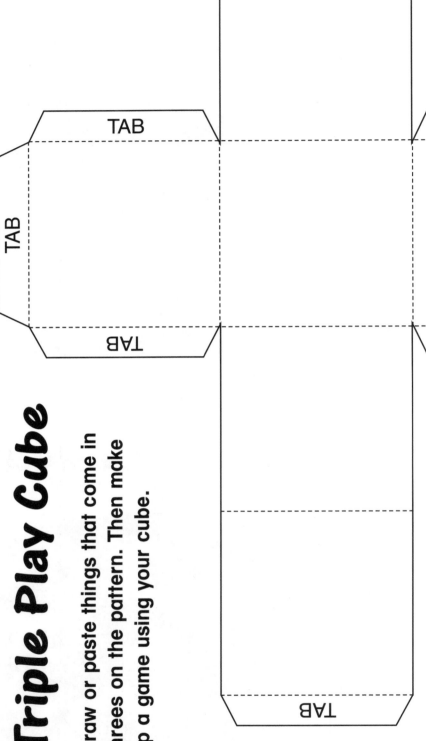

Draw or paste things that come in threes on the pattern. Then make up a game using your cube.

TAB

TAB

TAB

TAB

TAB

TAB

1. Cut along the solid lines.

2. Fold along the dashed lines.

3. Paste or tape the tabs in place.

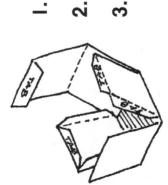

Name _____

1, 2, 3... Skip-Count!

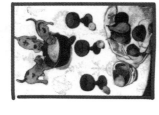

Paul Gauguin painted *Still Life With Three Puppies*. There were three puppies, three apples, and three goblets in the painting. Learn to skip-count by twos and threes by using the boxes below.

1. Continue coloring in every other box below. Copy the numbers under the boxes you colored onto the lines. Read the numbers and skip-count by 2!

1	2	3	4	5	6	7	8	9	10	11	12	13	14	15	16	17	18	19	20

_ _ _ _ _ _ _ _ _ _ _ _ _ _

2. Continue coloring in every third box below. Copy the numbers under the boxes you colored onto the lines. Read the numbers and skip-count by 3!

1	2	3	4	5	6	7	8	9	10	11	12	13	14	15	16	17	18	19	20

_ _ _ _ _ _ _ _ _ _ _ _ _ _

Just for Fun Turn your paper over and skip-count by five. Then try skip counting by ten.

La Piñata
by Diego Rivera

La Piñata   1953, tempera on canvas, 97 x 171½ inches

Let students celebrate art with artist Diego Rivera's rich, colorful painting, *La Piñata*. Young children easily identify with both the festive mood of the piñata play and the range of emotions expressed on the subjects' faces. This masterpiece easily connects with themes children know while taking them to worlds yet to be explored.

NOTES ON THE MASTERPIECE

La Piñata features a star-shaped piñata hanging above a group of children who are waiting for the goodies to fall from inside. One child with a stick is hitting the piñata so that it will open. There is a boy crying in the background being comforted by a woman. Rivera often painted subjects that dealt with the everyday lives, customs, and history of the Mexican people. The triumph of good over evil is symbolized by the breaking of the piñata. The treats symbolize good. Piñatas were usually made from a clay pot, but now they are usually made from papier-mâché. They come in all shapes and sizes. You may see piñatas at children's birthday parties and special celebrations in Mexico. The mural *La Piñata* is located in the Children's Hospital of Mexico in Mexico City.

Discussion Springboard

Display the poster with the reproduction of *La Piñata*. Conceal the title of the art with sticky notes. Have children look at the reproduction and share their personal responses to the artwork. Encourage observations with open-ended questions such as:

* What do you see?

* What do you think the children are doing?

* What do you think the round object is?

* What is falling from the piñata?

* What do you think is on the ground?

* Why is one child blindfolded?

* It looks like the children are having different feelings. Can you name some of these different feelings?

* Why do you think the child is crying?

* Where do you think this picture takes place?

* How many children do you see in this reproduction?

* Discuss the clothes the children are wearing. Do you ever dress like that?

* Would you like to be there with these children? Why or why not?

* What do you think the name of this masterpiece might be?

Record all responses and observations on a large piece of chart pad paper. Reveal the title of the artwork as printed on the poster. Then add the actual title of the artwork to the top of the chart paper. Display the chart paper alongside the poster. Use highlighting marker or tape to highlight key vocabulary words (for example, *children, piñata, feelings*). Encourage children to refer to it as they write in their art logs. Conclude this session by sharing with children any information you have gathered about this art masterpiece and related works.

Portrait of the Artist: DIEGO RIVERA

Diego Rivera (1886–1957)

Diego Rivera was born in 1886 in Guanajuato, Mexico, and was part Native American, Spanish, and Portuguese. His twin brother died in infancy. Rivera's artistic talents were evident at a very early age. In his home he had a special room where he could draw whatever he wanted; his father covered the floors and walls with canvas.

Rivera is famous for his great murals. His paintings usually told a story. He was interested in politics, the military, all people, and his homeland, Mexico. He painted many portraits and self-portraits. Rivera made sketches, painted in oil and watercolor, and created frescoes. A fresco is a special technique where paint is applied to a wet plaster wall, thus becoming part of the wall when it dries. Throughout his career he was influenced by different artists including Cézanne, Goya, Picasso, and Renoir. He experimented with different styles such as Realism, Cubism, and Surrealism.

1886
Diego Rivera born, December 8, in Mexico

1906
received scholarship to study art in Europe

1929
married Frida Kahlo

1931
one-person exhibit opened at the Museum of Modern Art in New York

In 1906, Rivera headed to Europe, where he learned from the great masters. By 1913, Rivera was experimenting with Cubism, a form of modern art where the subject is abstracted and geometric shapes are used to show things from more than one view. By 1918, Rivera had returned to a more realistic style.

As part of a new education program in Mexico, public buildings were to be decorated with murals. In 1922, Rivera painted his first mural, *Creation*. Once, while working on scaffolding so he could reach all the areas of the mural, he fell off and hurt his head! His murals were realistic so everyone could understand them, even if they couldn't read or write. Rivera's murals took many months and sometimes years to complete. He wasn't paid a lot of money to complete these huge murals in Mexico so he sold his artwork as well. Rivera was married several times. In 1929 he married Frida Kahlo, with whom he remained for most of his life. She, too, was an artist.

About this time, Rivera's art was becoming known in the United States, and he received numerous commissions to paint murals throughout the country. He was offered a one-person show at the Museum of Modern Art in New York. Attendance was record setting!

Rivera designed Anahuacalli, which was to become his home, museum, and tomb. It eventually held his large collection of about 60,000 pieces of pre-Columbian art. He was installed as a member of Colegio Nacional and in 1950 he was awarded the National Art Prize by the Mexican government.

Rivera's wife died in 1954, and he died on November 24, 1957. His collection of art and pre-Columbian treasures were left to the people of Mexico.

1942
began construction on Anahuacalli

1950
awarded the National Art Prize by the Mexican government

1953
painted *La Piñata*

1955
went to Moscow

1956
returned to Mexico

1957
Diego Rivera died

Curriculum Connections

 ## Mini-Book (LANGUAGE ARTS/SOCIAL STUDIES)

Use reproducible page 59 to create a mini-biography booklet about Diego Rivera. Read the information to children. Distribute copies of the booklets and help children fold their booklets along the dotted lines as shown in the diagram. Read the text through again, then invite children to add illustrations in the spaces provided. Suggest that children share their mini-books with family and friends.

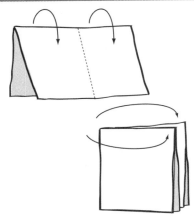

 ## Poetry Prompt (LANGUAGE ARTS)

Surprises

Surprises are round
    Or long and tallish.
Surprises are square
    Or flat and smallish.

Surprises are wrapped
    With paper and bow,
And hidden in closets
    Where secrets won't show.

Surprises are often
    Good things to eat;
A get-well toy or
    A birthday treat.

Suprises come
    In such interesting sizes—
I LIKE
    SURPRISES!
                —*Jean Conder Soule*

The poem "Surprises" can be used to help children explore the role surprises take in their lives. Before sharing the poem with the class, ask students to tell about surprises they've received and about those they've helped to plan. List their responses on a large piece of chart pad paper. Then read the poem aloud. Read the poem again, this time asking children to close their eyes as they picture the imagery suggested. Ask children to tell if the poem helped them to think of any more items to add to their list. Then copy the poem (two lines per page) onto large sheets of drawing paper and have children work individually or in pairs to illustrate the lines. Bind the illustrated lines in sequence into a book. Use gift wrap to create a cover for the book.

✎ Show Your Feelings (LANGUAGE ARTS)

Look at the reproduction of *La Piñata*. Although some of the subjects' facial expressions cannot be seen, certain emotions are evident in many of them. Ask: *What are the different emotions that you see in this artwork? Why do you think the artist painted some of the faces without features? How can you tell if a person is happy? scared? excited?* Ask children to tell if the face is the only part of our bodies that we use to communicate feelings. Have them use just their faces (or body parts other than faces) to demonstrate fear, anger, embarrassment, pride, joy, boredom, surprise, or shame. Challenge children to think of other emotions to mime for their classmates.

✎ Piñata Prose (LANGUAGE ARTS)

Have children write a story about what is happening in the painting. What are the children doing? Where do you think they are? To spark imaginations, provide the following sentence starters for children to choose from. Be sure to allow for students' own ideas, too!

> A piñata is a fun way to celebrate a special occasion. For a special occasion I would like to...

✳ The children are eagerly breaking open the piñata. If I were there...

✳ When I broke open the piñata you would never believe what came out. It...

✎ Papier-Mâché Piñata (ART/MATH)

In Rivera's painting *La Piñata*, the children are surrounding the piñata full of candy and fruit. It might be fun for the children to make a piñata together.

You Will Need: balloon ✳ newspaper ✳ flour ✳ water ✳ large bowl ✳ spoon ✳ pin ✳ paints ✳ paintbrushes ✳ crepe paper streamers ✳ wrapped candy ✳ dried or wrapped fruits ✳ small toy favors ✳ string ✳ stick or bat ✳ paper plates

Steps:

1. Blow up a balloon (adult only) and tie it shut. Cover a workspace with some of the newspaper.

2. To create the paste for the papier-mâché, mix flour into the water in a bowl until it forms a creamy consistency. Inexpensive, commercially prepared pastes are also available.

3. Tear strips of newspaper and dip them in the paste solution. Use fingers to wipe off excess paste. Cover the balloon with a few overlapping layers of newspaper strips, leaving a 2-inch opening near the balloon knot.

4. Let the piñata dry for a few days at least. When the newspaper shell is dry and hard, pierce the balloon with a pin and remove the deflated balloon from the piñata shell. Dispose of the balloon properly.

5. Paint the piñata with bright colors and decorate it with streamers.

6. Fill the piñata with treats. Hang it up and have children take turns swinging a stick at it in an attempt to break it open! **Keep students at a safe distance as each child attempts to break open the piñata.**

 ✳ Have children classify the candy or fruit in groups they choose (for example according to color, type, flavor, texture, size, or shape).

 ✳ Have children brainstorm different ways they might divide the treats fairly among all members of the class. Vote on one method to try.

Uno, Dos, Tres...Count!
(LANGUAGE ARTS/MATH)

Diego Rivera was born in Mexico. The native language there is Spanish. Introduce counting in Spanish to the children. Use reproducible page 60 to help the children remember the Spanish numbers. Cut the words out in English and Spanish as well as the correct amount of dots and tally marks. Glue them into the correct number box. The numbers presented on the activity go up to five. You may want to continue up to ten: (1) uno, (2) dos, (3) tres, (4) cuatro, (5) cinco, (6) seis, (7) siete, (8) ocho, (9) nueve, (10) diez. Some students may be able to speak Spanish fluently. Invite them to share a few words as well! Use your new counting vocabulary to count the number of streamers hanging from the piñata or the number of children in the *La Piñata* reproduction.

Indian Influence (SOCIAL STUDIES)

Many Mexicans have some Indian or Spanish heritage. Rivera had both! Two of the best-known Indian groups were the Maya and the Aztec. Rivera designed his home for his idol collection in a Maya-Aztec style mixed with his own. Learn more about the Maya or Aztec civilizations. Provide children with general information and invite them to create a museum corner in the classroom by lending books, toys, clothing, souvenirs, and artifacts from home. Use sticky notes to create descriptive labels for each "artifact."

Self-Portrait Power

(ART/SOCIAL STUDIES)

Diego Rivera painted many self-portraits. Sometimes he even painted himself right into a painting of a group or in a mural. In his mural at the Hotel del Prado, he painted himself as a young boy among many other characters. (He also put Frida Kahlo in the painting.) In another mural, painted for the Mexican holiday Day of the Dead, he put himself in the crowd of people. He had a tremendous talent for self-portraits, and his portraits showed strong personal resemblance.

You Will Need: free-standing mirror ✳ paper ✳ crayons, pencils, pastels, or paints ✳ paintbrushes ✳ yarn, paper scraps, and fabric scraps (optional) ✳ glue ✳ scissors

Have children take turns looking into a mirror (to note details). Then have them paint or draw a self-portrait. As an extension, provide assorted material to enhance their self-portraits, such as yarn, paper scraps, and fabric scraps. Children should know that a self-portrait need not be an exact duplication of the way they look. Instead, it can be an interpretation of themselves. **Remind students that mirrors are made of breakable glass and should be handled with care.**

Self-portraits

Celebration Mural (ART/SOCIAL STUDIES)

You Will Need: long sheet of mural paper ✳ crayons ✳ paints ✳ paint brushes ✳ glue

Diego Rivera is well known for his fabulous murals. Create a class mural by taking turns adding to the work or divide children into small groups and create a few murals, each on a specific celebration or theme of their choice. Rivera's murals were often frescoes, but your murals may be painted, colored with crayons, or decorated using collage. Let children design the work, and all you need to do is clear some prime wall space for the display.

More Ideas to Try

✳ Rivera experimented by mixing sand into his paint for added texture to his paintings. Try mixing sand or other materials into paint for different textures and effects. What does the paint with sand look like when it is applied?

* Learn about Mexican traditions. Discuss some holidays you celebrate. Have a fiesta in the classroom!

* Look at another work by Diego Rivera, *The Tortilla Maker*. Try making and tasting tortillas. Sample and discuss other common Mexican foods.

* Visit a travel agent and collect travel brochures highlighting Mexico. Invite a travel agent or class parent to visit and speak about Mexico.

* Learn to speak some Spanish words. Invite a high school Spanish student to teach the class simple vocabulary and phrases.

Culminating Activity

Display all four reproductions (or those you've studied together). Review the art and artists so children become reacquainted with the names and titles. Have children look at the pieces simultaneously. Compare and contrast the works of art. What new information was learned? Discuss artists, techniques, and subjects.

Book Breaks

* *Diego* by Jeanette Winter, text by Jonah Winter (Alfred A. Knopf, 1994). This book, written in English and Spanish, tells about the life of Diego Rivera.

* *The Tale of Rabbit and Coyote* by Tony Johnston and Tomie de Paola (G.P. Putnam's Sons, 1994). In this version of a Mexican folktale from Oaxaca, the coyote is tricked by a clever rabbit!

* *Borreguita and the Coyote: A Tale from Ayutla, México* by Verna Aardema and Petra Mathers (Alfred A. Knopf, 1991). This Mexican tale from Ayutla shows how a sly little lamb outwits a coyote...for good.

* *Let's Go: A Book in Two Languages* by Rebecca Emberley (Little, Brown, 1993). Each two-page spread highlights a particular place to visit where various objects are identified in both English and Spanish.

* *Celebrations* by Myra Cohn Livingston and Leonard Everett Fisher (Holiday House, 1985). This book of poetry highlights holidays celebrated in the United States.

* *Feelings* by Aliki (Greenwillow, 1984). Using everyday situations and fun illustrations, children can learn more about feelings as they read about and discuss the various situations presented.

Rivera is famous for the great murals he painted on building walls. His art was for everyone to see and enjoy.

When he was only three years old he drew a train with a locomotive and a caboose! Draw your own train in the frame below.

In many of his murals, Rivera painted scenes from Mexican life. Draw a mini-mural on the wall that tells about your life.

Diego Rivera
(1886–1957)

Diego Rivera was a famous Mexican artist. As a young boy, he earned a scholarship to art school. Later, he went to Europe to study art.

Name _____

Uno, Dos, Tres...Count!

Count to five. Learn how to count to five in Spanish.
Fill in each number box with all the ways you can show
that number. Choose from the boxes below.

1	uno	one	
2			
3			
4			
5			

1	uno
2	dos
3	tres
4	cuatro
5	cinco

Word/symbol boxes:

uno · one I

four	two	three	tres	cuatro	
•••	••••		II	••••	

₩	III	five
dos	IIII	••
		cinco

Teacher Resource List

General Information and Biographies

A Weekend With Matisse by Florian Rodari (Rizzoli, 1994). Also available in this series: da Vinci, Picasso, Rivera, Renoir, van Gogh, and Velazquez.

Pierre-Auguste Renoir by Ernest Raboff (Harper & Row, 1991). Also available in this series: Chagall, da Vinci, Dürer, Gauguin, Klee, Matisse, Michelangelo, Picasso, Raphael, Rembrandt, Remington, Rousseau, Toulouse-Lautrec, van Gogh, and Velazquez.

Getting to Know the World's Greatest Artists: Paul Gauguin by Mike Venezia (Children's Press, 1992). Also available in this series: Cassatt, da Vinci, Klee, Michelangelo, Monet, and Rembrandt.

Eyewitness Art Series: Monet by Jude Welton in association with The Museé Marmottan, Paris (Dorling Kindersley, 1992). Also available in this series: Gauguin, van Gogh, and Manet.

Famous Artists: Monet, An Introduction to the Artist's Life and Work by Antony Mason (Barron's Educational Series, 1995). Also available in this series: Cezanne, da Vinci, Michelangelo, Picasso, and van Gogh.

Pablo Picasso by Ibi Lepscky, illustrated by Paolo Cardoni (Barron's Educational Series, 1984). Also available in this series: *Leonardo da Vinci*.

Key Art Terms for Beginners by Philip Yenawine (Harry N. Abrams, 1995)

Art-Inspired Children's Picture Books

Dinner at Aunt Connie's House by Faith Ringgold (Hyperion, 1993)

A Painter by Douglas Florian (Greenwillow, 1993)

The Art Lesson by Tomie de Paola (G.P. Putnam's Sons, 1994)

I Am an Artist by Pat Lowery Collins (Millbrook Press, 1992)

Linnea in Monet's Garden by Christina Bjork (Raben & Sjogren Books, 1987)

Matthew's Dream by Leo Lionni (Alfred A. Knopf, 1995)

Visiting the Art Museum by Laurene Krasny Brown and Marc Brown (Dutton, 1992)

Camille and the Sunflowers: A Story About Vincent van Gogh by Laurence Anholt (Barron's Educational Series, 1994)

Children in Art: The Story in a Picture by Robin Richmond (Ideals Children's Books, 1992)

I Spy a Lion: Animals in Art devised and selected by Lucy Micklethwait (Greenwillow, 1994)

Poetry Collections

Celebrating America: A Collection of Poems and Images of the American Spirit compiled by Laura Whipple (Philomel, 1994)

The Sweet and Sour Animal Book by Langston Hughes (Oxford University Press, 1994)

Who Has Seen the Wind? An Illustrated Collection of Poetry for Young Children compiled by the Museum of Fine Arts, Boston (Rizzoli, 1993)

Software

With Open Eyes (Images From the Art Institute of Chicago)

A Is for Art, C Is for Cézanne: Fun with Images from the Philadelphia Museum of Art (1996, Philadelphia Museum of Art)

The Louvre Museum: Museums of the World for Kids! (coproduction of Voyager and Gallimard Jeunesse)

Notes

Notes